A
BODHISATTVA'S BUSTED TRUTH

Latif Harris

Browser Books Publishing
San Francisco

Copyright © Latif Harris

Front and back cover photographs by © Latif Harris.
Illustration on pg. 65 by Kumar Lama
www.tibetanpainting.com

ISBN— 10: 0-9772212-1-0
ISBN— 13: 978-0-9772212-1-9 – Paperback

ISBN—10: 0-9772212-2-9 –
ISBN— 13: 978-0-9772212-26 Hardcover
Library of Congress Control Number: 2006922220

Harris, Latif William
1940–

Published in 2006 by Browser Books Publishing
2195 Fillmore St., San Francisco, CA 94115
www.browserbrooksonline.com

For Alpha and Raphael:
Without whom nothing is possible, and to Steve Damon,
a patient and visionary editor

THE NUTS AND BOLTS

I wish to thank all the kind editors of little mags, newspapers, cyber-mags and chapbooks, who kept me hanging in there, waiting for an editor to pick up on my work for a serious book. In particular, I wish to thank Tracy Thompson for publishing my first poem in his mimeograph mag, *SUN, 1960;* Larry Goodell for publishing my first book, *u/c DUENDE PRESS '65;* Tisa Walden for publishing two of my chapbooks in the early 80's, and for her incomparable work as the editor and publisher of *DEEP FOREST.* She did much the same thing City Lights had done in the 50's, publishing more than a hundred titles by many of the poets whose work would not otherwise have been published. Her dedication to the group of poets whom I consider my peers, is truly remarkable and will not be forgotten. I wish to thank James Boyer May, who published six poems in *TRACE, Spring/66,* the most important literary magazine on the West Coast for two decades. Boyer May was the most active editor of West Coast writing, long before the beginning of the Beat generation. Unfortunately, he is seldom mentioned for his vision and accomplishments. He published a *Bibliography of the Beat Generation,* in TRACE 34, *Winter 1959.* He was far ahead of other editors of the revival movement. He recognized the importance of Kenneth Patchen's work, collected and published many reproductions of Patchen's original prints, and was the first editor to see an early version of *HOWL.*

Boyer May was instrumental in my endeavor as the founding editor and publisher of ANTE magazine in 1963 where I discovered the joy of finding and publishing young poets. Some of those I published in ANTE were david sandberg, Ronald Bayes, George Hitchcock, Diane Wakoski, Pierre Seghers (trans: D.M. Pattinella), Alvaro Cardona-Hine, Earle Birney,

Charles Bukowski, Stanley Kurnik, William Pillan, Gene Frumpkin, Dalene Young, James D. Houston, Ed Bullins, and Norm Moser. Many of these poets have gone on to receive international recognition, especially Buko whose grumpy, down and out, outlaw style was the antithesis of the *peace and love* generation. He was the hard-boiled L.A. character out of an earlier time who appealed to readers all over the world.

When I became involved in editing and publishing in the mid-Sixties, there were very few poets who performed their work. There were just a few who had published significant books, including Gary Snyder, Robert Creeley, Charles Olson, and Michael McClure. It was still a small community in 1960. The vast majority of active poets who created this movement showed up in Berkeley in July, 1965 for the poetry conference at the University of California. For the first time I met many of the poets whose work I had been reading. In many ways, this was the single most important gathering of American poets ever held. The workshops, daily readings and featured evening readings, plus the gathering of the community of poets at large was followed by a new national interest in poetry. Over the next ten years even unknown poets like Richard Brautigan became well known literary figures. The long years of publishing small chapbooks was followed by a deluge of books published by established New York publishing houses. Public readings began to draw huge audiences.

Today, in San Francisco, an underground of unknown poets perseveres; there are at least four or five daily readings in "The City of Poets." The public reading of poetry is the best way to get to the "music" of a poets work. The evolution of poetry as a performance art grew from the multi-dimensional "happenings" of Merce Cunningham, John Cage and others. The Troubadour movement was revived. The performance of the word changed the way poetry would reach the public. Bob

Dylan and Leonard Cohen sang their poems. The improvisational element of modern jazz became a natural part of the poet's composition and performance of a very new kind of writing. Even the chants or mantras from Eastern cultures entered the singing of the words.

Thanks to the editors of *Poetry Flash*, the newspaper of "The City of Poets" for keeping up with the innumerable readings, reviews, publications, and special events in the poetry of the West. I have read my poetry more than a hundred times in the Bay Area, and founded the Bannam Place poetry series in 1983. Bob Kaufman did his last reading there. Some of the others who read were: Jack Hirschman, Howard Hart, H.D. Moe, Kirby Doyle, Kaye McDonough, Kush, Tisa Walden, Gerald Nicosia, Neeli Cherkovski, Rosemary Mano, Paul Landry, Sarah Menefee, and Ron Kovik. The Bannam series was the last North Beach reading series that had a distinct affiliation with the early jazz and poetry readings that happened there.

A core group of poets who came together at Bannam Place, provided the impetus for the Silver Anniversary Editon of Beatitude, edited by Jeffrey Grossman. This magazine, with a long history is open to anyone who would like to edit and publish under the name *"Beatitude."* The origin of the word beatitude is open for discussion, but the beatific openness of mind best describes what has happened to many whose roots are bedded in the rich soil of a tradition that began here long ago.

TABLE OF CONTENTS

III. An Unfinished Life

PREFACE

In Search of the Marvelous

I wrote my first poems at age twelve. Thanks to the kindness of two librarians at the Rosmead branch of the Los Angeles public library, who continually put my poems up on the bulletin board, I was "hooked." Those poems kept me coming to the library and took me to a retreat beyond the wasteland of G.I. tract homes proliferating in suburban Los Angeles where I grew up in the forties and fifties. I loved the library, the smell of books, the rows and rows of stories waiting there every time I visited. Even the wax on the floor had a smell I cannot forget. Just thumbing through huge tomes in languages beyond my comprehension, filled me with the possibility of a future beyond boundaries of any kind. I knew where I was going. In my graduation yearbook I said that I wanted to be a writer and travel. And due to great good fortune, I have traveled far beyond anything I could have imagined at such an early age.

1

Unfortunately, none of these early poems have survived. This selection of poems written between 1960 and 2005 is like a map of my inner life, which constantly rubs up against the reality of times high and low, times of sadness and great joy. The images come from my lifelong search for the "marvelous" as described by the French Surrealist writers.

I did not know there were other living poets until about fifteen, when I heard about the wild things going on in San Francisco. I had been reading Lord Byron, Thomas Love Peacock and some Whitman, though at that age his work did not seem like poetry to me. I thought all poets were dead! I know the ones we read in English classes were. Not long after hearing about living poets in San Francisco, I was very fortunate to be sent there by the Navy, and spent a year on Treasure Island. The view of the City from there was phenomenal. On liberty I would get over to North Beach where, when I was eighteen, I met Allen Ginsberg at The Coffee Gallery. He was somewhat famous already due to the publication of "Howl" and all the uproar created by the profanity trial that followed its publication.

During the next couple of years I met most of the poets connected with the "Beat" scene. I also met *one* Robert LaVigne, the painter, who Ginsberg later referred to as the "Court Painter" of the Beats. Robert knew all the poets of the San Francisco Renaissance. LaVigne, whose body of work is formidable, has remained a friend for almost 50 years. He is one of our greatest living painters.

He also introduced me to the work of John Wieners, whose "Hotel Wently" poems, printed by Auerhahn Press with design and line drawings by LaVigne, blew my young mind. That book of poems became the standard by which all poetry, including my own, would be measured. Those few poems written by a very young poet, and the poems of "surrealist" poet Phillip Lamantia -- who, at the age of 15 was recognized by Andre Breton as an authentic voice of surrealist poetry in America-- I continued to read over and over. I would go to the work of these and other poets, and like a musician, I would play the music of their poems to help me open the channel for my own work so that it could take shape and come through. Other times I would discover poems "waiting to be written" in the images of my dreams.

Another technique, which I found helpful, was going to a friend's art studio to watch him go through the alchemy of putting paint on canvas. I found certain pieces of music might release the poem, which had become like a headache. I always felt closer to painters than to poets. Robert LaVigne, Gordon Wagner and Nick Nickolds are the painters with whom I spent the most time.

I must give thanks to Howard Hart whom I met in Mill Valley in 1975. I was having a little gathering of poets weekly at a used bookshop. One night Howard walked in just as I was reading Phillip Lamantia's "Hermetic Bird". We had never met, but he had been very close to Phillip in New York, and I think we both knew that this meeting was fraught with blessed figurations. We spent a lot of time together for the next 20 years. Howard's long time connection to music and to jazz musicians gave him an extraordinary ear and helped him to write lyric poems of great beauty. Howard had close ties to the surrealists, and taught me to trust immediacy.

Surrealism, as I came to understand later, was a natural way of receiving and expressing things that come from the unconscious, dreams, lines written on fences, or even partial dialogs heard while riding on a bus. Also, as you will see in my introduction to the "Surreal Dohas," a similar method was used by Buddhist *tertons* who experience direct reception for writing spiritual songs, poems and teachings. In my generation, the search for living spiritual traditions like Buddhism, and the use of hallucinogens to break through the everyday illusions of some codified reality, opened up a whole new field of perception. Many of these poems were influenced by a combination of things that were a part of this unique historical period, an expression of a time by a person who was on a "bus." There were many busses zooming around between 1960 and 1975. The bus became a symbol for the vehicle in which a group of like-minded individuals travel on a certain mission or path.

So here is a rough chronology of my life during that time: I stayed in the San Francisco Bay Area from 1959 to 1963; returned to Los Angeles and founded the literary magazine ANTE, 1963-65; met Robert Creeley at the big Berkeley Poetry conference in Berkeley in the Summer of '65 and went to New Mexico to study with him until

1967; spent the Summer of 67 in San Francisco; back to New Mexico where I finished work on my BA; stayed briefly at the commune New Buffalo north of Taos on the Rio Grande; returned to Los Angeles where I opened a small head shop/bookstore 67-69; went to England to do graduate studies at the University of Essex 69-70; moved to Amsterdam, stayed on the road heading south to Rome, making forays to Greece and the Near East; returned to United States, Mill Valley 1972; made a pilgrimage to Java, Indonesia to study with Pak Subuh, founder of Susuli Buddhi Dharma; lived in Marin County until 1976; took refuge in Buddha Dharma with His Holiness Dudjom Rinpoche; was off and on the streets of bitter dreams for the next five years; moved back to San Francisco in 1978 where I worked with the surrealist and performance artist Gordon Wagner 78-83; pretty much traveled in concentric circles for the next ten years.

Since 1981 I have lived with my wife and soul-mate, Alpha, whom I met while working (and living in an upstairs loft) at Browser Books, which I helped Steve Damon renovate when he bought it in 1981; I returned to work at Browser in 1997-98 after my second bookstore failed in the Lower Haight. And now, in 2006, a large circle is making a temporary closure as Steve has asked me for a book of my poems to publish in his new publishing venture: herein it takes life.

In these poems you will see the names of cities and towns that I have visited. Traveling, being in motion is like following, or marking a literal path, which is scratched into the geography and geology of places one visits. These experiences are etched in the heart and mind to become a resource, which would not otherwise be experienced. Visiting cultures that have almost nothing in common with each other or with my own, I have found a commonality among disparate peoples. It is important, however, to see that this "commonality" does not include those few, who have or exercise power, and whose self-centered thirst for power is the overriding fuel for "their" bus. They have, for the most part, cut themselves off from the symbolic cells of their own cultural roots.

But I am an American Buddhist, and taking on the trappings of another culture is something my Lamas warn against. I write from my experiences of growing up and living in this culture with all its faults, gadgets and technological wealth, and no matter how much I might wish I came from another culture, or pretend to act like someone from another culture, this is where I was born and this is the one that hangs around my neck, and is where I practice Buddha Dharma. Buddhism is another of those "buses" I ride on, and those who ride with me are my *Sangha* brothers and sisters.

Three things came together for me in the mid-Seventies. I was doing Jungian therapy and did a session of automatic writing everyday for about two years. I used my work as a poet and my dreams to delve into my inner self, and my pronounced anima driven archetypes; I took refuge in Buddha Dharma from His Holiness Dudjom Rinpoche; and I began to trust the surrealist tendencies in my writing. Later I would learn about the cycle of "dohas", or immediately received and transcribed songs or poems practiced by a few extraordinary Tibetan Lamas. The forward to the Doha section goes into more detail about this technique.

I offer these poems to all beings as a map of my journey through this lifetime, and hope they will be of some benefit and joy to those who read them.

Latif Harris
San Francisco
February 15, 2006

I.

BETWEEN SLEEP
& AWAKENING

SELECTED POEMS

ONE MORNING

&so there we sat
  high on dharma
    &telegraph hill
      talking of death

&moldy leaves
  &wind &tugboats
    &watching Berkeley
bare a new sun
brilliant &naked

re-planning yesterday
  &forgetting today
    an impossible task
      &walking back down to earth

&waking up with them
  in the streets on streetcars
    &riding through the day

forgot the beginning
  &it became yesterday
    as will tomorrow
      &next week

      &forever
North Beach 1961

11

ON AIR

I've got to write my things

on the window panes

translucent as

warm kisses

clear as lips on iced glasses

not a shadow exactly

like a red fingerprint left there

like a bi-valve sea creature's cilia

quiet out there

poets on air

WEATHER REPORT

o.k. let's go

let go the lines

holding the ship at bay here

o.k. let's go

out into the storm

peaceful seas please

those or these

unable to leap

into an unknown

like sheep

stay put

NOTES OF BLUE SAGE

Recognized it at the Timbuktu Trail
flying eagles and One Eyed Jacks

    north of the twin peaks

atop the adobe Kiva
when my ochre bones
are done to dust
let them whip up

    like a lovers lust

the sun's splash at dawn
in the Great River
refreshing us at New Buffalo

nude each morning
light of the male sign

penetrating the Rio Grande
urging up from the cold well
    of civilization
      a bell sounds
        we eye the vestibule

of a very high desert

YOSEMITE

Toast for breakfast
or toadstools and moss
          for the hungry ghosts

with log-headed tree trunk bodiless skins
floating around in the mists of falls

they are the Mother and Daughters of Tenaya
who is Chief of the walking sleep
they live in the atmospheres of this valley
and they do not salute Captain America
nor his legions of carbon monoxides

they come down from Tenaya's canyon
and will bend like bows around our trespasses

COYOTE SEEN

As space curves
it must eventually come back
to meet itself
wherever it began
it will also end
which is back where
it begins again
coming upon that coyote
alongside the wet mountain road
with it's heavy silver-gray winter coat
slicked by
s
   n
     o
     w

      f
      l
      a
        k
      e
     s
we know we must meet him again
at this same spot
at the end of that

l
o
n
g

s
l
o
w

c
u
r
v
e

just as the light bends
traveling with us
like the headlights of the car
minus its speed
striking coyote's eyes
it reflects back hitting our eyes
and I know with certainty
all those things we've seen together
will repeat over and over
no matter how deeply
or in what shade
death shall finally freeze us

ICONS OF REPAIR

"It is not enough to cover the rock with leaves
We must be cured of it by a cure of the ground
Or a cure of ourselves,
That is equal to a cure of the ground,
A cure beyond forgetfulness
The fiction of the leaves is the icon
Of the poem, the figuration of blessedness
And the icon is the man."

- Wallace Stevens

1

There are memories that lactate
through the eyes
behind the eyes

brimming with icons
of former lives

like light sealed in fossils
within a damp ancient wall
leaking out around the edges

it is the color of milk
seen through a thin slice of white opal

he turns his head
slightly to the right
and sees the messages
tooled in Paleolithic rock
his head like a hammer

strikes the pillow
           with the first rays of dawn

           2

It is upon him
like an endless flight of mallards
stretching along all the days of Autumn
over the tulip fields of Holland

it is upon him
with more power than ever before
it reaches down through him
like very slow motion lightning
kicking on the stars

it is upon him
like an answer to the question
he had ceaselessly recomposed
walking with the hands of his sons
held tightly within his own

it is once again upon him
like feinting into strength
leaving a meaningful trail of shadows
whose imprints are valleys of commerce
valleys of trees and rock
valleys of sand moved by wind
valleys he has walked
 holding tightly the repetition of lines
in the palms of his children's hands

            the lines he passes from his father
                and all the fathers that stretch back

like an endless flight of mallards
stretching along all the days of Autumn
over the tulip fields of Holland

                3

His disillusions began unwinding
like a wrapper around common coins
he held his head up
and yelled at demons traveling
unconcerned through the house of dreams
where is the roof he cried
these libraries these broken mechanical things
these crawl spaces
hallways and marble stairs
these precious and wholesale episodes
are dingy
where is the roof he cried
the light the air the distant blue stars
this house is a suicide note
a trembling flyleaf in an open book
where is the roof he cried

                4

He played certain overtures
on the strings of his strength of youth

sometimes disguised as a swan
            at others as an armed demon

he wrapped and repelled until
he became both full and empty

then divining the mood of the crowd
                    like a minstrel
moved on

the dream began to bend
back on itself
repeat itself through sick contours

                5

Within himself
soft armor pierced
by the morning wind

she bends over him singing

the loons along the bank
watch the colored balls sink
            one by one
into the mossy pockets
        of the green felt lagoon

the prehistoric wizard
with the eyes of a shark

the lizard
        in a suede suit
            stands waiting for his shot

6

He wore his animal skins
    until he wore the animals thin
wearing down all things
he could not otherwise control
    sometimes for pride alone
did he drop a large chested buffalo
    then in thundering herds
drove them from the plains for good

having leveled the living top
he drilled below into the living past
pulling up the liquid fern and flesh
        and firing it once again
            put on ancient animal skin

7

By the poet
days dull and sharp as a thorn
beneath a yogi's rock seat
admonishing clusters of wasps
    swarm above his head

22

he loiters in the mechanics of night

you can see him limping
along darkened streets

or striding high moonlit mountains

how many times does he turn
    at the moment of pleasure
        to deeper darker thoughts

toward the ultimate dark door

framed in opal light

he feels in all pleasure
a sudden gasp of doom

he sometimes lies frozen
        within the small tributary of his life
like a giant headed carp
with black and gold eyes

8

Tapering down engulfed in paper weights
his solid dreams of tropical medicines
harbored in the stomachs of eels
wind blows up the corners of uniformly
psychiatric concerns ramble like flicked eyes

flames purse their lips defiantly

in the critique of his fantastic mind

in the basement of scientific tomes
Blake hands him a large and heavy key

razzle-dazzle tics and foot tapping
arched his back and smiled

9

Losing track of dates like hoof beats
comforted by the blue springs
centered in a small circle of green
mathematics spring up here
in conversation among camels
he passes through many lands
in search of his own face
listening
listening
salaams and goodbyes
he sits in crowds
beneath the folded flaps
of empty tents

he is no great man
sitting beside the weathered bent men
arriving hollow eyed from long journeys
through the numbing passion of their lives
he sits among them like a crystal

vibrating

among them as a traveler
listening
listening
listening
once again
it is upon him

10

He activates the sky
        with copper rods

now absorbing the shock
like waves of delight

small puffs of cloud
crisscross the eyes

like backbones curving
        in solid sleep
like an x-rayed bank
        of dozing crocodiles
on the blue sands of the Ganges

four sharp jolts
before the heart loosens
and falls from the fourth floor
injuring several turbines
passing below

UNTITLED

On the edge of obliteration
clouds white as sheets of lacquered chalk
reform the sky

me at the door that will not close

navigating through the human ritual

                which will not close

mouth ajar
like a pelican's
just as it hits the water

standing by the door of your body

opening and closing
      defiant and uncertain
              as solid space
is full and empty

desire comes and goes
    like Bedouins
      traceless
           catafalques

of passing days
    and places

perhaps yellow dried gardenias
still scented
    will call

and time once again
    will stand
        aside

ALL YEARS FIRST

the New Year
no one on the lagoon
but us gliding
with water birds

on the high tide
at noon
conversation light
as the wind

metaphor of four oars
propelling us far out
from the shore

the brittle racket
of a distant Kawasaki
draws lines of sound

down the middle of Highway One

    - New Year Day 1985
      Forty-fourth Birthday

CORPUS dna/lsd

Prelude to the spiral framework
denuded

the elemental
              so far
structure passing along

eye color
      nose shape
          density of hair

flame of imagination

            then
into a moving collection

called body
      baby
child
      young man
adult
      old man
shriveling body
      death
dust
      memory
time
  is left
for the descended ones

FOR NERUDA

"Heido marcando con cruces de fuego
El atlas blanco ? tu cuerdo"

I have gone marking the atlas
of your body
with crosses of fire

I have loved even the bitter veins of the pomegranate
I discover rediscover Eluard
in you

how to live
on water and love and poetry

Was that today I went
out with you
in a morning rain
was it not rather
a year ago

It's the larger voice
in me wants out

the history of my
cells decay
like scales on a fish
    like the skins on a onion

I study love
    everyday
        like a Rabbi

PROBABILITY

There is always cat litter
and Greece and sick Sappho
hanging with a litter of cats

in the Buddha's time
it was

and High Flying Athens

and the law school witless bookmen
who know nothing of dogs
nothing about them
or cats or light sockets
or odes to lovers
or fuses or a child's eyes

wide with joy seeing Papa
turning into the driveway
the probability of another writing
of this poem
        is very unlikely

SANTA DOMINGO

The cottonwood dolls dance
with the doughboys

      slanting left
hopping up right

the art of it
        slick as a fleece of seeds
beneath my feet

a demented morphology
provide the wings

way up here
   where the air
      always sings

SEEN IN RELIEF

Pablo Neruda I have worked
to uncover the commonality
of unseen things
roots reach down into the cracks
like dendrictic reflections of leafless trees
into ponds of half conscious matter
these politics
these politicos

pimple-faced sadist
cover us
with their fecal shadows
hacking heads off
after the struggle
the Serpent Bird forgotten

Quetzalcoatl forgotten by them
remembered by you
whose tongue forms vowels
with which the bird speaks

of a long history imbedded in rock
and of the ragged flesh
in the leaves of newspapers
and burning books

I have always seen them there

       likewise
           in my gardens of light
half of you there

WORDLESS LOVE

You found me like a pebble
which one collects from the beach

like an odd object for which
no one can find a use

like seaweed on a sextant that's run aground
like fog on the window
          which seeks entry
like the jumble in an unmade hotel room
the wastepaper left at the intersection
          on the morning after the feast

a traveler sitting on the ladder
          stepping off the train without a ticket
a stream diverted into the field of the low life riverside
dwellers
a beast out of the wood
          trapped in the headlights of a car

like a night watchman coming down
          from his rounds into the stale morning
like an un-dissolved dream
          in the dark shadow of prisons
like the panic of a bird blundering in a house
like a red mark on the ring-finger of a betraying lover

a vehicle abandoned in a wasteland

like the bits of a letter
   scattered in the windy streets
like the tan left on the hands
   after a summer has passed
like the lost look of someone
   who realizes he is lost
like the baggage left standing in the train station
   unclaimed
like a door or perhaps a shutter
   rattling somewhere or other

similar to the mark left on the heart
   by love at first sight

a stone marker along the road
marking the loss
of a loved one
like headstones of forgotten soldiers

like the color of a bruise that does not go away
like a useless siren of a singer
   far out
like the scar left on the flesh
   long after the cut of the knife

like an escapading horse
   drinking from a stagnant pond
like a pillow flattened by nightmares
like an insult to the sun through fractured eyes
like anger which sees nothing
   as the sky has changed

You found me among the books
        like a word you can't take back
like a vagabond who falls asleep
        in a sweet smelling barn
like a dog wearing a collar with no tag
a man from another past
crackling with anger and static

like a bolt
        looking for a nut

you took
        me in

EVERYDAY DREAM

I have been visiting the worlds
between sleep and awakening

the worlds of vapor trails

                     and watermelons
salt air and acacia

where intellect surrenders to curiosity
all her rigid demands

sounding a soft hammer
                  against a bell

a bell which will not sound

a bell whose resonance
         resides in the dawn

I have been visiting the worlds
of a thousand islands
strung together like beads
                  encircling the languid heart of a
leopard
which contains photographs
of distant planets
        with violet mountains and orange skies
I have been out there so long
that maps have begun weeping

blistering noons
     frozen in the rings of Bristlecone Pine
arboreal quills stopped in mid-air
like bolts of green lightning

intransigent as a porcupine
       yielding as a woman
made of water and air

invisible as the print of a sparrow's foot
on a frosted piece of white marble

I have been out there so long
that the rescue has become unnecessary

the drone of helicopters has settled down
                 with the bees
the shouts of the rescue party
     are drowned by the leaves
in the domain of morning
when activity replaces me
I will fall asleep
on a carpet of dark dreams
and barter within the bark of trees

SUR SUITE
--For Alpha

The round berries fall like feet
on the soft white sand

you remind me of the quiet
and I can hear it
as clearly as I heard the ocean
only a moment before

The spouting of whales goes up
like umbrellas in a Spring rain

you said tell me if you see any whales
and there they were
        filling the ocean
in a line close to the shore

The length of the day
is not quite constant
despite our measuring device

the fennel I picked to sweeten
the air in the car
        and the time it took
are inconsequential
        and immeasurable
as a kiss on a Jim Dine heart
succulent as rock
sometimes seems

galloping in a field of blue wheat
in the low tide
      when its jaded sides
      show

they look as soft as
the bodies of green horses
with the lather of the sea
pouring from them

everything migrates

      transforms
          circulates
becoming much alike

a horse
    rock
field and sea
      whale
          wood ducks
     you and me

Big Sur 1983

FOR RAPHAEL

I been livin' every limping day
      sixty-two years by the way
side by side and far apart

makin' love
killin' things small and smart
and pounding at the art of the word

the only door there is

two sons dead
gone on ahead

Raphael Karim
holds my hand here
for the other two

Just when I think
I'm a Bodhisattva
the cup looks empty

to me

the Lama taught heart to heart
until he looked just like me

the tea cup turned over
like some refined mystery
and he left me hangin'

in a sky with no trees above

an empty mirror

left me whistlin' Dixie
a lovely melody
not at all where I thought

I'd be
                facin' sixty three

TARA HERE AND THERE

The silence of early morning
is broken by
a small baby sneezing
in a room high above the street
once twice three times

my mind on Arya Tara
my root erect in her heart
of glassy air
this is everything!

everything filling no thing
insistent effort of whispers
die down

the thin wall between them
and me
between she and me
grows thinner than
      old documents

the passage of her leaving
tears away like wallpaper
the knock
at my door
erects my spine

ON LADDERS OF AIR

Starlings descend like a shower of stars
the higher I climb
        the further they fall
cormorants
            gulls
                grebes

and flouncing sea lions bark
sliding in and out
of red velvet capes
stitched by dinoflagellates

down there she looks like Victoria
in that grandmotherly pose
we all know so well

I hear her talking to them

shoo she
        shoo she
                shoo shree
lapping up the shore

This ladder I climb
disappears
sinks down into
reflecting kivas
ups away from the peppers
and husked corn

stacked on circles
of cinnabar and ash

up like a flash
through the smoke hole

A DASH OF CLASH

Dolomite morning
Turandot turning

      la-la la-la la la la

syllables of Tibetan

Om Benza Sato Hung

naturally rising speech
unlike operatic laughter

ha-ha-ha ha-ha ha

In
a e i o u

the armature of all energy
is charged

WHAT

Heard in the wind on Hopi Mesa
during Healing Dance

The words trance-alluvium
bonedust leached from the ground
lingua in the lingo of the organism

leaf rot around the corn mound
first word grain through neuron
pushes up through the throat
to sound

heals all illnesses

ha ha ya ya ya
ho ho ha ha ha

bells and shells ring a ling
the couple's arms surround the Medicine Man
he blows a cloud of corn pollen
into their ills

tomorrow all will be well

LINGO ONE

Fresh rose on ivory
hands of ebony in flight
across an unreasonable
wine colored sea
said the poet of rhapsody

epic toning of unfinished bells
Homer
       Homer had his ear
         to the ground

rosewood lines the cabinets
where sound is kept
a tumbling act of clappers
in the adepts hands of poetry

LINGO THREE

"I got used to the elementary hallucination"
-Rimbaud

I thought I heard her say
     reality is the toy of chance
quoting something the poet said
the night before last

often I hear what I hear
and not what is said

The gold diggers passed this spot
and shot at the owl
shouted like mad men
when one of it's wings came loose

Yes
   Sir America
my people
will make trouble for you
    and your people
       said the chief of the grizzly clan

when I am dead I will call
all my people to come
and they shall hear me in their sleep

oh I have promises to keep
    and reality is the toy of chance

washrag of gray and white damp clouds
squeezed dry over the granite ridges
protruding like knuckles and fine bones
up from the flat hand of the yellow meadow
where a great gray owl rotates his head

his yellow eyes peel back the grasses
great wings spread and he's gone
gliding away without a whisper of sound

the sound of motors
the swish of tires throwing up water
then absolute silence

is this a highway

transfixed by this vision
we dive into the moment like swimmers
at once a part of the water
flesh liquefied and bones elastic

we will float off like a fish sideways
like a manta through the kelp

if only I could move all the tenderloins
to this spot
all the slums and racketeers
prisoners and their guards
city editors
entrepreneurs and sailors

if only I could bring them to this spot

I thought I heard her say
    reality is the toy of chance

the morning rain has stopped
vapors hang at the sides
of the igneous armor
worn by the Chief embedded in the
    ground clouds rising
guarding Citadel of the valley
like gauze torn from the chest
of a three thousand year old mummy

give me your cup
before it runs away

we are dancing on the brink of a world
mad

we are humming an old tune

often I hear not
what is said

PILLOWS

I knew immediately what you meant
words like pillows
each word like a pillow
arranged to suit our heads
and
rearranged into phrases of comfort
and
arranged again when they go flat
and once again when our sleepless heads move

Our minds like large beds
contain all the pillows
we can imagine
words to name things
like hand and hypothetical
we are senseless without words

to comfort us
our heads spend so much time
resting on these pillows
Coleridge slept with *Observations on Man*
under his pillow

We bolster ourselves with words
and pillows
our thoughts oozing into the feathers
along the rim of sleep

IN THE NILE OF YOUR THOUGHT
lsd/dna

The rock tower which rises
                    from an invisible sea

is filled with red-haired women
                    hearing voices

the liniment of somber onyx
against the dour skin of remembering

cats carved on your forehead
above the ancient eyes of Egypt

at the mouth of the Nile

where does it end
in the quiet river
in the Nile of your thought
in a crocodile's heart

we were stoned
                    walking
near the Ponte Vecchio

we talked of certain premonitions
concerning the flight to Istanbul

discovering later
the medicinal benefits of uva ursi

the root of the dandelion
and mandrake in somatic cartoon

lysergic definitions

extraterrestrial silhouettes

alloy of mind and word
silicon layered
between blood vessel and sand

chemical phrases charging
through the mute celled fingers
like a cello

hand plied to hand
body to body
electromagnetically wedded

the men on ice
          la mere docile
silent as air
notte dolce adesso

the rain on your feet
splash of cognac
my arms slide down your sides
surrendering to gesture
the adamant gesticulations
of disconnected hands
forming mudras from which

those women's voices
echo the name of Psyche

this rolling preoccupation with Eros
winding down silver threads
floating in dark clouds
the moonlit arms of Seraphita

the half-closed eyes
        galloping along the edge
            of a turbulent river

the Nile
        where crocodiles slept

INVENTION FOR TOM BURKE

Poised between the thighs of history
an unnamed bird
with black and white feathers sits
like an unrevealed onyx

calls my name of earth and stone
calls my name of moon and star
calls to me in Latin and Hebrew

cakes the cells of my body with desire
named at dawn between the pillars of fire
falling in the celestial downpour of stars
naming the bird that waits
beneath my name of plungers
calling to him squeezed by her
shadow and living body entwined
traces of finger and beak
on the back

phrases of bloodsick love
lovesick blood
of word and name of nameless
wonders edging up the erect spine

1973 Mill Valley
Sits on Tom's desk

ETRUSCAN BLUES

Mist condenses on strings
of an artificial harp
as each moment passes
on its way to oblivion
Etruscan blues detain the muse
outside the town Sienna
a string of silver beads slide
back into the red earthy
where Dutch calliopes steam
whistling anthems
of sunflowers and crows

- Florence 1970

FOR 'POETS AGAINST THE WAR'

Homage To Sam Hamill

The politics of Holy Dharma
has reared its Naga's head

in this time of the gyring wheel
Dorje Drolo and Vajra Kilaya
we call upon you
as if you were our policemen
coming to arrest the bad guys
to cut through the density of no thing

My loved ones
there is no one who knows the pain
more than you or me

two children struck down by alcoholic-drug demons
two younger brothers slain by AIDS

cancer in the air
it is everywhere
crawls on my skin

We give money prayers
　　　　practice kindness
and generosity

there is no limit to the asking
only in the giving

We are broken down and the wheel has spoken
a spoke has busted
bringing us down in a New York minute
dropping broken towers on us

no time
　　　is not a time
　　　　　like this time

It's such a wonderful joke
told again and again
from the beginningless beginning

This is the Bush'age
the Kaliyuga Waltz
bombastic reactionary waltz
in four/four

FOR ROBERT LaVIGNE ARTIST

Visiting you after many years
in this dreadful time
remembering my youth and the highway

you showed me beauty
your palette brimming with color

being young and handsome
I thought we would change the world
with brothers and sister on the same cue
bringing down Sol to light our joints

In a whiff more than forty years have passed
we have lost so many
to Wall street to the Mission/Bowery sidewalks

born to die
the only secret Buddha gave his followers

When I saw the tons of human ash pour
from those extravagant Towers burning
I thought of The Hanged Man
The Tower
and less arcane things like my breath
so precious and frail
my Heartmind turning to you
and all my wise teachers dying daily
In Iraq and Liberia

death is no more brutal
than dying in ones own bed
but it is so mindlessly planned by human hands
by moguls of many skins
in red white and blue houses
in red white and yellow shacks
they steal the breath of children
who've known not a moment of beauty
or a full belly
or a day free of fear

We did make changes
in the physics of paint and word
co-opted by those who steal it all
sealing the fate of so many
with Human bombs and
beneath the sophisticated fallout
from "smart" bombs

Bush is not alone
his are not the only bloody hands
          on the turning wheel
            of this bizarre life

Dear friend Robert
it is so good to know you again
these things fulfill those prophecies
we saw coming

SATTY

Who died from a fall in his studio
During the great San Francisco Floods
Of 1981/82

Terrestrial commotions
the rain moved earth
removes bridges over which we walked

there is no life in death
but before and after
there is something

There are ladders we climb
and ladders we go down

there is this coming and going
through the passion of our lives
through the baroque rooms
through the bodies of lovers
through unlit tunnels
through meadows of iris and larkspur
through the eyes and hands and ears and mouths and
noses
through that wall of visible death
that invisible demarcation   where

but for a moment we lose our balance
    and fall into the big net of memory

get to catch the aerial bicyclist

gliding back and forth
        on a thin cord

stretched above the breathless crowd
    safely grounded
        on the bleachers
            in the Big Top

Satty was a great collagist
Author of "Cosmic Bicycle"

OLD SPOONS IN THE RUINS
external sobriety

For My Gone Son Simon

The whack and crackle bolts of silver lightning
and boom of electrified air
                              applauds
the rainbow over Downeyville

a big cedar split
        beside an upside-down
            smoldering steer who'd sheltered there

twenty years post-lysergic definition
        this reality
            this vision
                we saw rounding
                    a slow curve in the road

I loved you
        together we
            in the rain of Mother Sierra

lotus land of Orgyen
garden of mental Eden

    I am shattered
                by your sudden death

II.
DOHAS OF
A SURREAL LIFE

Dedicated to my Precious Teacher
His Holiness Dudjom Rinpoche

And all the kind Dharma Friends
Who have tirelessly pulled me along with them
On the Path
In the empty field of no harm

Homage to Samantabhadra
The primordial Buddha "Ever Excellent" May my
presumption to share my "bizzy-dizzy" mind be of no harm

INTRODUCTION

Dohas are sacred poems received by a few Tibetan Lamas, who are incarnations of previous Lamas and "Wisdom Holders." Some of these realized beings are called "Tertons" or treasure finders. My root lama, His Holiness Dudjom Rinpoche, was the reincarnation of the great 19th Century Terton Dudjom Lingpa, and was in a line of succession which goes back to Guru Rinpoche (Padmasambhava) the Buddha who brought Buddhism to Tibet. These treasure texts, or termas, were hidden by Guru Rinpoche himself as teachings for a future time.

Some of these treasures were placed in holy shrines called Stupas, others are found hidden in caves, or in the crevasses of rocks, and even at the bottom of lakes. Some treasures come directly to the Terton and are called "mind treasures" usually received as dohas. It is said that these great *Terton's* can directly receive several teachings simultaneously, and dictate them to any number of scribes at one sitting. My precious root guru His Holiness Dudjom Rinpoche revealed thousands of lines of these treasure texts.

I do not pretend to see these poems of mine as anything more than writings of a very ordinary person who has had the great good fortune, or karma, to have been born in the right world, at the right time, and found the right teacher, and with the right motivation to have received teachings of great Vajrayana masters, while living a quite wild and sometimes wonderful life.

In the poems I refer to as *"Surreal Dohas,"* they were received often while on retreats, or as images from dreams which had a powerful effect on my mind upon awakening, but they have also come to me in the normal ups and downs of an ordinary life. I have seen how, no matter what I am doing, I can hear the music of ancient Tibetan masters in the mantras and dohas I have repeated millions of times. You will see in the brief quote from the great Master and poet Saraha, also called "The Great Brahman," that I appear to have borrowed the first two lines outright in several of my own poems. But I find upon looking at my lifework of more than 1,100 poems, that these ideas are a recurring theme in my poetry. I have heard this particular teaching so many hundreds of times, it is only natural that such lines would "pop up" like hot toast as I go about my ordinary occupations.

This a short stanza from one of the glorious writings of Saraha which addresses "Cutting through Resistance" from his *"Song of Esoteric Instruction:"*

Listen! do not regard cause and results as two
There are no causes and results which arise as
substances.
If this yogin's mind is maddened
By the mind which hopes and doubts,

The co-emergent pristine cognition will be bound therein. *

I have been assured by some of the great translators of Tibetan, that it is impossible to translate the beauty of Saraha's poetry, or the "Dohas" of any of the great masters into English or any other language. Mostly we are left with ideas, but the music is missing.

Knowing a little about the life of Saraha is also very instructive when I look back on my own life and see how accomplishment is often a great "illusion."

In a time when Buddhism was on the outs in Brahman society, Saraha studied with many great Buddhist and Brahman masters, including those who taught Tantric doctrines. In the daytime, he practiced Hindu teachings, and at night he practiced Tantric Buddhism and drank wine. This was strictly forbidden in Hindu society, so Saraha was put to several tests by a great king, which he passed because of his knowledge of Buddhist Dharma. After seeing the results of these tests in which Saraha practiced the weaving of magical illusions, including drinking molten copper, the king said that anyone with these kinds of powers can drink wine if he wants to. The king bowed to Saraha and asked him for teachings. So he sang the three cycles of Doha.

Saraha took a young wife and went to a quiet place where he practiced meditation. His young consort begged for food. Once Saraha requested that she make a dish of radishes and yogurt. She placed it before him but he was in a state of meditation, which lasted for twelve years. When he awakened he asked her where the radishes were. She replied that he had been in a "trance" state for twelve years and the radishes were removed long ago.

Then Saraha said that he was going to the mountains to find an isolated place to meditate. His young wife replied that moving the body to an isolated place is not necessary, but "the best kind of solitude is for the mind to free itself from ordinary names and concepts. You have meditated for twelve years and have not freed yourself from the idea of the radishes!"

Seeing this was true, he abandoned the world of illusion and attained enlightenment through the gift of Mahamudra. In Tibetan Buddhism he is considered one of the Eighty-Four great Siddhas or masters of the Tantric tradition.

* Nyingma School of Tibetan Buddhism (vol.1)
by Dudjom Rinpoche (Jikdrel Yeshe Dorje) p.335
Wisdom Publications, Boston 1991

THE VIEW

Do not become bound
by hopes and fears
regarding this practice
we call life and death

effortlessness is the key
not accomplishment through
practice and head banging

give up your attachment to all
but the view

and then
                 give that away too

BODDHISATTVA'S BUSTED TRUTH

I cannot write anymore until I write this:

with thirty five cents in my pocket
overdrawn checks floating
at George and Arni's grocery
(food for the kids)
K & L liquor
innumerable   watering   holes   which   shall   remain
anonymous

it is the nature of the game of being a poet
and WANDERING raggedy Nagpa Buddhist
the grinding poverty of it
was like swimming in tar

you can only swim out so far
before you must reconnect with land
if you do not make this periodic contact
with the ground
likely you will drown

(The Dark Ages 1978-1983)

74

GOODBYE RETURN

For Aram Simon
April 1, 1969 - April 8, 1990

In The Name of
Buddha, Dharma and Sangha
I pray

let that day go
                there is
no stopping it anyhow

dear Son gone away with Morpheus
that angel of long
                long
                        sleeps

you shot up
and bang
your heart stopped
and your eyes bulged
and you followed Him
joining that long line
ahead of you
                moonwalking

your first word was
                moon
as we stood there
looking out over the Aegean
in that little town near Ephesus

75

in the Autumn of your second year

you wanted always
so much to live
at the cliff's edge over the black water
and you did

before tumbling
through the eye of a needle

Namo Lu Med Ten Gyi Gonpo Lama Khyen

The favorable conditions for rebirth
are difficult to obtain
our bodies are so precious and fragile

do not linger in the terrifying realms for long
I've made a place for you
and will wait for your return

AVALOKITESHVARA

Wine drinking insight
Sweet Water Bar
Mill Valley 1977

Prevaricators blockade themselves
against a thousand arms
swerving from her like a garden
overgrown and dim

He toils within her who is lost in vigils of alcohol
unable to speak
uneasy
refusing the temptation to pull out
of this condemned place

Malaise rises from all the flesh
like a terrible fever
transmigratory fishes wash up on the strand
where the newborn struggle not to return
raised by his toil
wrapped in her arms

OM BENZRA SATTO HUNG

I repeat over and over wishing my condemned friends
    a peaceful mind
        or oblivion
            during these dead years of awakening

I say to them eye to eye
with all my heart

May all The Buddhas
    in all the realms
        forever shine from the rainbows in your eyes

ON SIXTIETH BIRTHDAY

At the Browns'
Mendocino Coast
Quarter moon above

   below

       the Orange-Billed Oyster Catchers
          snug in down coats among hard rock

     2001 metronome still ticks
         does not stick as they said
onward

melted blue deity flicks itself
into my left eye
momentarily blinding me

with molten lapis
of the Medicine Buddha

my 60th birthday comes and goes

I ride the wingless Iron Dragon
completing one great cycle

         rusty now
           but with lusty dreams
at dawn my Beloved Dakini
with White Tara eyes

smiles in her sleep
assuring with her warm breath

this amazing longevity
I've been given

12/31/2000

AMITAYUS

I count you on my Mala today
click
        click
                click

beads sliding in a whisper
along a string

praising you
            my vendor of a long life

Visualizing your form

Om Ah Mara Nri Dzi Wenti Ye So Ha

buzzing in my mouth
entry to the cave of my skull

Ye So Ha

Sitting on the moment of death every second
jerking along on the
                Samsara Trolley
called No Desire

Last night I awoke choking on my own vomit
unable to breathe
in a panic my thoughts did not turn to you

The Healing One

but to the invisible air
body sustaining air
death so near

Through your kindness
I breath again
allowing me to go
into the museum

 of my bizzy
            dizzy mind

HOW LONG WILL IT LAST

Disguised in the pale suit of my skin
I ask the Lama
How long will I live
Even desire has died in me

But not the Anger

        Rides me like a tiger

And harsh speech

        And jealousy

The MO
        shows one year

Practice Orgyen Menla
Remember Dorje Drolo's Mantra

Four years have passed
My rickety Dharma Practiced

How long now Lama

Oh a few more years he says
Many Lamas have been to the precipice

Forgetting the unreal
I go on "sun gazing"

Not unlike old geezers
Like myself
And my old friend Rick Fields

FOR ALL MY DHARMA FRIENDS

Homage to His Holiness Dudjom Rinpoche
I am humbled before your great wisdom

Rainbow in the West this morning
On Parinirvana of H.H. Dudjom Rinpoche

Jigdrel Yeshe Dorje
Himself a reflection of the Lotus Born One

Only later do I learn this
    (checking my Tibetan Calendar)
       my eyes filling with tears)

Lama of my Heart always seated there

Who 22 years ago gave me a refuge
Named me Orgyen Samten

As my bit of cut hair burned
My remaining un-hooded self
was reduced to a grain of blue rice

Followed the Dharma willy nilly
With billions of sentient beings
Through a billion universes

OF GREAT EMPTINESS
On the day you left your body
      Your picture on my shrine

Six thousand miles away

Toppled over

Three days later my Dharma Brother
Tells me what I already knew

That your suffering body
Went up in rainbows

Like the one I miraculously saw

This morning
So many years later

On the 18th Day 11th Month
Fire Mouse Year

WHAT WILL I DO WHEN MY LAMA GOES AWAY

What will I do when my Lama leaves
Weep
      fill with anger
           pity myself

Call to him from afar

No says the dream
In Milam Bardo

He is neither here nor there but in my heart
He was never elsewhere than there
And cannot travel beyond those boundaries
My boundless heart pervades

The meeting of emptiness and compassion
Sometimes I will sing to him
Spontaneous dohas of joy
Just as I do
While washing morning dishes

I will see him in the rainbows of soap bubbles
With my "bubble eyes"
As Tarchin-La says

I will see him in my pain and joy
And secrete him away

Until we meet again in some revolving future

Alongside a pond near a trail in the high mountains

Dedicated to Precious Lama Tarchin Rinpoche
Who's patience and kind abiding
Extended my time here

FLIRTATION IN BARDO LAND

Orgyen Menla hear my prayer

In no man's land
On Bardo Island
Light plays on the ripples
Of a river
Without
Banks

The pain not eased by morphine
Dreams of demonic nurses
Eight days in hell realm
Of a hospital bed
A hint of things to come

I must try to practice today
I see the face of Dudjom
Cannot repeat mantras

The man in the bed
Next to me groans

I am dying this minute
The powder of instability
Looks the same as yesterday
Just more pain
In the colon
Ruler of rotting body
Insinuates itself

If doesn't let up soon
I'll float out of this realm
Into the churning muddy river
Chewing away
On a small piece of ground
A stepping stone
To rebirth

DURING DRUPCHEN

Mind on Tara
from the front office

in the wake of a passing car
kicking up dust
busting my view in its shadow of rainbows

Even the dust
at Pema Osei Ling
has rainbows

Tara is reading an old book
of my poems
            weeping

written lifetimes past
sad and joyful verses

It makes me happy for a moment
but realize I was happy before
and now the evening songs of Swallows

I write contented
once again refuged'
at this sacred root place

of pure Dharma
  Where even the dust
      the shadows of last light
         transform into rainbows

Written at Pema Osel Ling
during Drupchen Retreat 1999

FORCE ZERO ROCK'N'ROLL

The Time has passed
I'm an old man now

alive within jags and crooked crags
of a life lived
                    half'n' half out

dipped drugged and stripped rugged

in his face
            the father

your face
            mother
                    not unlike my own

spaced from a thousand lovers

oh Bob
Dylan Thomas'
was almost someone else

music
thumbed around Ireland
to the high country

where my love waits alone
on a mudded path

where a pig repaired the Stupa
with a muddy bottom
and became a Buddha

OLD SUN GEEZERS

Latif searching for metaphors to
explain the path
at the speed of life
       Rick smiling

Lama Chozod teaches
about the innumerable
Buddhas that exist on the tip of a finger

I see the tail of that comet
they say
a million miles long
so
   very

      long

it seems

yet
     in Buddha dharma

it would fit easily
        into an ordinary suitcase
you wouldn't have to sit on it
to get it closed

you smile that smile you had
like loud laughter

crush an atom and kill
billions of sentient beings
in an instant

Paradoxes are crossed
by boats of light
tinted by the Lama's
compassion

and you said *Fuck Cancer*

YAB YUM

unseemly to lay on you
The cause of my unraveling

Blocking the flow of epinephrine
In a slosh of alcoholic demons
Running through my bloodstream

Your demands were beyond me
Beyond the groceries and rent
Beyond the Buddha realms
Beyond the bodies of lovers

Quieting the rage of my Dragon nature
I took so many

The kindness of women
Who saw me as a blessed Knight of Hearts
Orpheus for a night of love

The one who would come timelessly
Into their desire

It is so unseemly for me to blame you
But who held the key

And who had the lock
Which shackled us apart
When I came into that endless
Forest of lovely women

FOUND IN A NOTEBOOK DATED 9/18/98

No pleasure in this pleasure
this ephemera of no thing

no freedom in this freedom
this wandering in no place

the answer to knowing death well
is to disavow this ramshackle life
Guru of radiant speech

I reach out to you

my body a rented house

my mind
           a circumambulating guest

INKLING

Forget the *Two*

Mountain and Wind
    Body and Mind

The One seems so Substantial
    The Second Unseen

They are as Nothing
But Phenomena of a moment
Flashing on the Mind

Cultivate a Taste for First Things

Your big-hearted Guru
Sitting on your Head

Be glad you are Human
Not some god on a Golden Throne

All is not Permanent
        Not the Lake
                Not the Osprey diving

Be mindful
        Learn Skills
Got it?
Now let it
        Too

Go on the way

Do Good Deeds
  Ease the Way for Others

    Homage to Longchempa
    Bridel Vail Creek, June 1994

ANSWER TO AN UNGIVEN KOAN

Only a man capable of great love
and great sorrow
understands the inner laws of physics

The Twelve Stages
        of interdependent origination

which prevail in the heart
contain all theories
between birth and death

What do you say

SONG

Orgyen Trinley Rinpoche sang a song
as we drove North
on Highway 280

And then in spoken verse
I ask what does it mean
    he
        sang it once again

it means
gazing at the face
of the lama

and dissolution of the ground
into the sound
        of joyful enlightenment

like the unsurpasable one
          born
               through speedy transference
we practice
grow old and sick

then at the moment of death
with correct view
and understanding compassion
the Lama will hook the singer
and take him
    like a Dharma Friend

to vacation in a God's realm

sounds good until

the vow remembered that

he will be born again

WHEN A MAN SHOWS PLEASURE IN THIS LIFE

revealing a certain indifference
to death and birth
it becomes impossible for others
to embrace him

III.

AN

LIFE

IT ALL TURNS BROWN WHEN MIXED

So this is old age Poet
    or no

The sun is alive in its pink
and orange splendor

At the savage moment it
drops behind the flat sea

He falls into a lush wilderness
Where love survives like
a lost tooth
Among the bleached bones
in the dark green sea
Among the torpedoes and
shark fins

He is high and would
stay that way forever

Slipping in among the mollusks
Held together by a thin silver thread
He would take his place
in the lining of this poem

Between the conical breasts
of the woman he loves
Alongside his brothers
Defying the executioner
the net of his death

Thrown out into the sea
to snare the living

Spits back the bitter seed
He is bored and moves

from room to room
his slow rhythms are not cool
he walks back and forth
stumbling
on the slick cables of
loneliness

he is lazy
        drugged by
a rugged silence
    not crazy
      but iced
        only love

in its speechlessness
will save this man's life

analogs of feeling tumble into the work
his hands long to hold
a woman's slim waist
once again

in the finger paintings
   of his mind
        it all turns brown

GLIMPSES OF LIFE ON A SPIN
(An open ended, ever growing poem...)

Born breech on New Year's Eve
An angry man from underwater
Saint in the clouds waiting
Scorpio rising
Mars on ascendant
Eyes bulging from meat sockets

Georgia Boy
Raised in LA

Muddled through a typhoon in Japan
Food poisoned in Hong Kong
Spit in the Thames
Saw the weeping Christ leaning on a wall in Rome
Became laughing Buddha on peyote
        in Sandia Mountains of New Mexico

Ate rancid dog meat in Hong Kong
Faced the demons of the Dalang in Tjilanak Indonesia
Played Frisbee with Yale graduate on the beach
        of a small Turkish town near Ephesus
Fell down drunk in the Colorado Rocky Mountains
Crossed the Alps
Wept in the Vermeer room of the Rjiksmuseum in
Amsterdam
Ran into Artaud coming up from the Hague
Circled Stonehenge with my infant son Simon
Saw Arthur's grave in the West Country
Walked the suicide cables of the Golden Gate

wanted to jump many times

Looked up to see Heidegger floating
in the halls at Frieburg

Had Polio, cancer, pneumonia, ulcers, kidney stones,
torn cartilage, high blood pressure
alcohol poisoning, drug overdoses,
tonsillitis, headaches, bad disks in back
neuropathic interruptions, failing eye sight
ruptures, bruises, flues, cavities, paranoia,
depression
coronary arteries full of fat,
ectatic vessels, artificial knee, stroke in colon
and now the final undoing of brain shrinking
shaky limbs, psychic phobias

I am not a hypochrondriac,
I am not

I AM NOT A HYPOCHRONDRIAC

Lost two of my three sons,
Oh my

Raphael, my third son
has become a teacher of young children
and shares his wisdom
with all who know him
such a gift
remembering the insubstantiality

    of gifts
I duck at fly balls

Had spirited visions of a perfectly normal life
with a wonderful wife, two cats, and a light filled home,

freedom to travel the first, second, and third worlds

Been blessed by six great Tibetan Lamas,
    a sweet and mad yogi
       who called me a gypsy horse thief

Spent thousands of years in meditation
Spent millions of years watching television

Taught by young Turkish Mullah,
  an Indonesian Mystic
   who named me Latif,
    a Roman Catholic Priest
     and a Coptic Christian mystic
      with whom I smoked Kief

Took refuge in Buddha Dharma with His Holiness
Dudjom Rinpoche
Finding the way and the view
a suit that fit well
but needs pressing from time to time

Visited half-dozen various medicine men,
peyote visionaries
seen junkyard saints,

pointed out to me as Bodhisattva's
from a Bodhisattva poet
not afraid to work hard
and carry water

Saw the Pope at a distance, became a friend of Bill W.,

Fell off a 200 foot cliff at twelve
        landed running in bloody circles
            concussing

as my short life flashed clearly
in consciousness which came and failed
at a billion frames per millisecond

Saw a vacuum cleaner turn into a lion age four
Cursed, blessed, complained, wept, laughed, sighed
kicked, been kicked, hit, been hit, bit
been bit, cursed, been cursed
spit at poets, been cold cocked by poets
begged and ignored beggars
saw the coming of the Millennium
hoping the computers might actually cease to function
for some unknown personal quirkiness of mind
which I have always honored

Said to Grace Slick in Sweetwater Bar
in 1977
Grace in Deed!
    and she took a swing
        missing my point and my chin

Visited Guru Rinpoche's retreats in Bhutan
circled the holy places
where the Buddha taught

Prayed in Gaudi's Cathedral of the Sagrada Famalia
the sacred family

In Yamika repeated mantras
   placed my hands on that wall
      that vibrates
         hums a universal hum
So much more, the dreams, the shadows
you know
         you all know what I mean

I am

Just like all the red-blooded American males of my
generation

in a huff of mental insanquinity I wrote the following

It does not help me to hear that my poems moved you
you who were so sure of yourself in tagging my corpse
with carnations wired to my little toe

you whose legs refuse to open to my pencil
the subject of my inquiry resolves in spending the flesh
wearing Cotes du Rhone slippers
pulled by a fast boat
I want to go home with the Armadillo

to the country music of Amarillo
and where in the world is that English Girl
I promised to dine on
doves alight in the dust of morning
the pulse peels away at crumbling piers
grebe gulls cormorants bark of sea lion
mother of the shadows
her red dress of plankton
billowing at the surface
like a giant placenta
ocean sea
   ocean bay
     inlet cove
The pulse of bay tide
peels away the crumbling piers
the higher I climb
the further they fall

grebes gulls cormorants bark of sealion
mothersea in her red dress of plankton
billowing at the surface
like a giant placenta

ocean sea ocean bay inlet
   our language becomes a chant
I have repeated myself many times
in this work

   is anyone paying attention
we hear the universal conversation
it penetrates us through speech

the slap of waves on the bow

shoo she shoo she shoo she

it penetrates us with sound
squawks, squeaks, whistles, chirps
the sound of the mourning dove's wing
as it comes and goes

the welder's torch the carpenter's hammer
the backfiring motorcycle
roosters squabbling
the parrot yelling for his mother

I peel away like the crumbling piers,

    everything peels away in mindfulness

the mind whips around like an unthreaded movie
projector
showing no film
    but that which is that

and what's more
you hurt me so bad
oh baby so bad
'nough said

FIN TEMPORARIA

Note from the Publisher

Browser Books has been a leading literary bookseller in San Francisco since 1976, devoted to offering carefully selected titles in a friendly, welcoming atmosphere. One of our main interests has been in the literature of the sacred traditions of the world, from East and West, and how this literature can support contemporary women and men in their search for meaning in their lives.

Through the years we have continued conversations with others who share the same need for such a search. Many of our customers have come to rely on us not only for our selections of books but for our shared interest in how these books can be of help in their lives.

We have decided to take this conversation to a new stage by entering the world of publishing. If you are interested in joining this conversation, you should know that we are now accepting manuscripts of poetry and prose devoted to the search for what has often been called *awakening* or *transformation.*

For more information on submission guidelines please visit www.browserbooksonline.com or email us at Browserbooks@aol.com. Or you can come by and visit us at 2195 Fillmore St. in San Francisco.

300 copies printed in Electra Lt Std
with 26 lettered copies hardbound with jacket
signed by the author.

Photos on front and back covers taken by author at
Lopburi Ruins, Thailand
*Showing the exquisite among impermanence looking up
and looking down.*

Browser Books Publishing
San Francisco